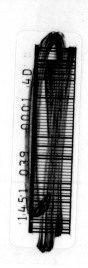

THE LEAVES OF AUTUMN
An Oneida Indian Legend

Retold by Ellen M. Dolan

Milliken Publishing Company, St. Louis, Missouri

Library of Congress Catalog Card Number: 87-61658
ISBN 0-88335-587-6 / ISBN 0-88335-567-1 (lib. bdg.)

I am Tenskwatawa, the storyteller.
Come and sit around the campfire to listen.
This is a story about the leaves of autumn.
It is told by the Oneida people.

Near a forest was a large Oneida village.
Many people lived and worked there.
At one end of the village,
there was an old woman's lodge.

The woman was so old,
no one remembered her name.

Many in the village had forgotten her, and she spent her days alone.
The woman sat and watched the beautiful butterflies.

She loved butterflies.
They were her friends all summer.

3

Only the village children cared about the woman.
They often came to see her and called her the story lady.
She knew of things that happened long ago.
The children loved her tales of mighty hunts and brave deeds.

The children also loved the story lady's candy.
She made it from maple trees in the nearby forest.

Each child had a turn to stir and taste.

The children laughed and played near the lodge.
But at the end of the day,
they went back to their village.
Then the woman felt very much alone.

Soon it was the time of the harvest moon.
The woman grew very quiet. In her heart was a secret.
She would not see the snow moon this year.
The Great Spirit would soon call her to his home.

7

The days grew colder.
The butterflies got ready for their long winter sleep.
The woman was sad. She would not see her beautiful
friends again.

The children were also getting ready for winter.
It was always a hard time for their people.
They helped cook food that
would last through the
cold days.

The woman did not put food aside.
She ate what she found near her lodge.
She did not worry about winter.
By then she would be with the
Great Spirit.

10

The children did not forget her.
"Thank you for the food, children," said the woman.

"But I cannot pay you for it.
I am old and of no use to anyone."

"That is not true," said the children.
"We learn much from your stories."

"Then I will tell you one more story," said the woman.
"It is about Little Frost Chief."

"Little Frost Chief comes from the Far North.
He is sent by the Great Spirit.
He comes when the time of the freezing moon is near.
Every step he takes leaves a tiny, frozen crystal behind."

13

"At night Little Frost Chief dances over the ground.
By morning he has left a blanket of frozen jewels.
We call it frost."

14

"The animals of the forest are wise.
They know the ways of the Little Frost Chief.
When he dances, they look for a winter home.
Many animals sleep all during the time of the freezing moon."

15

"Do you see this tree?
The butterflies have already made their winter homes here.
I shall never see my beautiful friends again."

"Why do you say that? Do not go away," said the children.
"Soon I will go to the Great Spirit," said the woman.
"Do not be sad. It is right for me.
Everything comes into the world and someday must leave again."

The children wanted to do something for their kind friend.
"Perhaps the Great Spirit will wake the butterflies," said one.
"But then they will die in the frost," said another.
"Let us ask the Little Frost Chief to help."

That night the children prayed very hard.
Little Frost Chief heard the children.

He wanted to help the kind woman too.
But he did not know what he could do.

Then suddenly Little Frost Chief had an idea.
He got cans of paint, brushes,
and a ladder.

He ran to the forest near
the woman's lodge.

Little Frost Chief worked quickly.
He went from tree to tree.

Soon the leaves on all the trees
were painted.

The Frost Chief used
beautiful colors: red,
yellow, and orange.

Little Frost Chief picked a leaf and blew on it.
It floated just like a butterfly.
Then it fell quietly
on the ground.
Little Frost Chief was
happy with his work.

In the morning, the children came to the lodge.
"Look at the beautiful colors on the leaves!
They look just like butterflies when they move.
Our friend will be happy to see them."

The children hid in the trees near the lodge.
"Story Lady, come out! Come out!
We have a surprise for you," they said.

"Oh, can this be true?" said the woman.
"My friends have come back.
I thought I would never see them again."
And to the woman's old eyes, the leaves seemed like butterflies.

The last days of autumn passed.
The woman watched
each leaf float to the ground.
She was very happy.

Then the freezing moon came.
All the beautiful leaves were gone.
And the woman was gone too.
She was now in the happy home of the Great Spirit.

Each year Little Frost Chief comes to paint the leaves.
Then we remember the kind woman who loved butterflies.
And we think of the children who wanted to make her happy.